SCjC
5-12

Grow Your Own

Tomatoes

Helen Lanz

SEA-TO-SEA
Mankato Collingwood London

This edition first published in 2012 by
Sea-to-Sea Publications
Distributed by Black Rabbit Books
P.O. Box 3263, Mankato, Minnesota 56002

To Carolyn—thank goodness your support is more reliable than my tomato canes

9 8 7 6 5 4 3 2

Published by arrangement with the
Watts Publishing Group Ltd, London.

Library of Congress Cataloging-in-Publication Data

Lanz, Helen.
Tomatoes / by Helen Lanz.
    p. cm. -- (Grow your own)
Includes index.
ISBN 978-1-59771-314-6 (library binding)
1. Tomatoes--Juvenile literature. 2. Vegetable gardening--Juvenile literature. I. Title.
SB349.L347 2012
635'.642--dc22

                    2011001222

Series editor: Sarah Peutrill
Art director: Jonathan Hair
Design: Jane Hawkins
Photography: Victoria Coombs/Ecoscene (unless otherwise credited)

Credits: Brian J Abela/Shutterstock: f cover b. Chrislofoto/Shutterstock: f cover t. Makai Dunne/
istockphoto: 23b. Leon Forado/Shutterstock: 7cr. Roman Ivaschenko/istockphoto: 27cr. Helen Lanz:
endpapers (2, 31), 13t, 25tl, 25tr. Lisa McCorkle/istockphoto: 6t. Penny Oakley: endpapers (1, 32), 22b,
25b. Francesco Ridolfi/istockphoto: f cover b/g. Ariel Skelley/Corbis: 3. Alexey Sokolov/istockphoto:
27b. Friedrich Stauss/Alamy: 18t. David Taylor/Alamy: 24b. Sophia Tsibikaki/istockphoto: 26b. Rob
Walls/Alamy: 23c. Every attempt has been made to clear copyright. Should there be any
inadvertent omission please apply to the publisher for rectification.

The author and publisher would like to thank the models who took part in this book.
Thanks to Jasmine Clarke and Tony Field for kindly sharing their gardening knowledge.

February 2011
RD/6000006415/001

Safety Notice:

Gardening is fun! There are a few basic rules you should always follow, however. Always garden with an adult; any pesticides and fertilizers should be handled by adults only and applied to specified plants only; wear appropriate clothing and footwear and always wash your hands when you have finished gardening.

Contents

Words in **bold** are in the glossary on page 29.

Why Grow Your Own Tomatoes?

Do you like to eat salads in summer? What are your favorite ingredients in a salad? Could it be peppers, lettuce, or perhaps tomatoes?

▲ *Most tomatoes are juicy and delicious in a sandwich or salad.*

▲ *Not all tomatoes are red; you can get yellow, orange, white, and even brownish-colored ones.*

Size and Color

Did you know that there are thousands of **varieties** of tomato? They vary in size from enormous beef tomatoes to tiny cherry tomatoes, and in color from yellow to red. Flavors vary, too. The small cherry tomatoes can be sweet tasting; some of the bigger varieties have a "fruity" taste.

Grow Your Own

Have you ever thought about growing tomatoes? It really is a great journey to go on, one of flavor, color, shape and size, and smell, too.

▲ When you water a tomato plant, it gives off an amazing smell.

◀ ▼ These are the main parts of a tomato plant.

Truss

Stem

Leaf

Flower

Fruit

Root

Root hair

Fruit or Vegetable?

A tomato is actually a fruit, not a vegetable, because it has **seeds** (see page 10). However, we think of it as a vegetable and eat it in salads.

Seed

Be Prepared!

You've decided to go for it. Growing your own is great fun. You will get plenty of fresh air and have the pleasure of watching something that you've grown from seed grow into something that you can actually eat.

Thinking Ahead

It's worth thinking about what you will need. For yourself, you will need some old clothes that your parents or carers won't mind if you get dirty, including rubber boots or old sneakers.

▼ You will *need* plant pots to sow your seeds in.

▲ You could wear gloves, but you don't have to.

You can grow tomatoes in containers, **growbags,** or a vegetable patch. If you choose containers you will need some **potting mix** and **fertilizer**.

▶ If you are growing in containers, you will need to feed your tomatoes with a liquid fertilizer.

▲ Try to get a growbag that is thick, with plenty of soil in it.

▶ You will *definitely* need some tomato seeds!

◀ Some types of tomatoes need support from canes as they grow.

Top Tip!

It's a good idea to keep a growing diary, writing down everything from the tomato variety to how and when you did things. This will help if you decide to do it again, and will be fun to look back on. If you have a camera, you could take pictures as well.

All About the Seed

There are so many different varieties of tomato, it can be difficult to know which one to grow. Use the Internet or ask at your local garden center for advice.

Tall or Bush Type?

There are indoor and outdoor tomato plants and two main types—cordon (tall) or bush plants. Cordon plants grow well in the ground or growbags, needing a garden stake, or tall stick, to help them keep upright. Bush tomatoes grow better in pots, or hanging baskets off of the ground because their fruit dangles down. As a beginner, it might be best to go for a variety that is **hardy**, or quite tough.

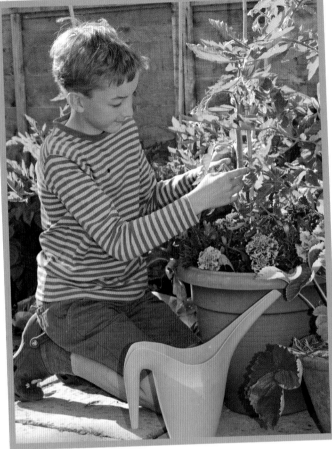

▲ You can expect to be picking your tomato harvest about 20 weeks after sowing your seeds.

SCIENCE SPOT — Seeds

Seeds are embryo, or baby, plants: inside the tiny seed case is all the information needed to grow into the adult plant. A seed waits until the **conditions** are right for it to **germinate**, or start to grow. It usually needs to be dark, damp, and warm.

Step-by-Step

1. You will need to start your tomato seeds off inside.

2. Prepare your pots. If they aren't new, wash them out so they don't pass on any **diseases** to your young tomato plants. Almost fill to the top with potting mix. Potting mix has a fine texture so your tomato seeds don't have to struggle to grow around large lumps of soil. However, you can "sieve" the potting mix through the holes in a plant pot to remove any lumps if you like.

3. Water and leave overnight—this allows the soil to settle and makes sure it is moist (slightly damp) for the seeds.

4. Space four or five seeds evenly in the pot. Lightly cover with potting mix.

5. Cover your pot with plastic wrap and place somewhere warm and sunny, such as a windowsill.

Encouraging Growth

Check your seeds every day—it's important to keep the soil moist at all times. Be sure to water the seeds evenly and don't let the soil get too wet, or waterlogged.

▲ It's fine to lift the plastic wrap to see if your seeds have started to grow.

Shoots

After about eight days, you should see little **shoots**. It's so exciting when you see a little green shoot appear.

SCIENCE SPOT *Germination*

Germination is the point when a seed starts to grow, breaking out of its seed case. The seed stays dormant, or asleep, until the conditions are right for it to grow. When the seed germinates, usually the root is the first thing to break through the seed case. The cotyledon, or seed leaf, also begins to grow, often becoming the first green leaves of the plant.

▲ Be patient! It may take some seeds a while to germinate.

Lots of Light

As the shoots start to grow, remove the plastic wrap. Make sure your **seedlings** are getting as much light as possible.

▶ A windowsill is a good place to put your seedlings.

◀ The seedlings will grow toward the light. You might want to turn the plant pot occasionally.

Top Tip!

If the seed "coat," or husk, sticks to the leaf, stopping it from opening properly, put a drop of water on the husk to soften it. This might help the leaf to push it off as it grows. Try not to pull it off because this might damage the leaf.

Pricking Out

▲ *This seedling has two proper leaves, with two more leaves forming.*

About two weeks after sowing, your seedlings will probably want more room to grow. When they have grown at least two leaves, move them to a 4 inch (10 cm) pot of their own. This is called pricking out.

Top Tip!

When the seedlings start to grow, choose only the healthy, strong ones to **plant on**. This means you have the best chance of growing healthy plants.

14

Step-by-Step

1. Fill each new pot with potting mix and water it, as you did before. Poke your finger, or the end of a pencil, into the soil in the middle of the pot.

2. Gently grasp one seedling by its leaves (not the stem, which might break), and lift it from its original pot. Or you could use an old spoon to scoop up a seedling, including some of the soil underneath it.

3. Place the seedling into the hole you have just made and gently, but firmly, push the soil around the stem.

4. Repeat this with your other seedlings. As they grow, space them out along the windowsill so their leaves don't touch. It's useful to mark each pot with the variety of tomato if you are growing different ones.

Preparing to Plant Out

▲ The clusters of flowers are called "trusses."

About a month after pricking out, when your plants are 6–10 inches (15–25 cm) tall, or clusters of flowers begin to grow, they are ready to be planted in your vegetable plot or growbags.

Hardening Off

It is a good idea to put the pots outside on sunny days and bring them in at night, to get them used to being outside. This is called hardening off.

Find the Right Place

Tomato plants like sunny, **sheltered** places, so make sure your growbag or pot is put in the right position. It is best to do this before you plant out your tomatoes.

▲ Make sure there are no more frosty nights before the plants are placed outside all the time.

Step-by-Step

Preparing a Growbag:

1. Be sure to give the growbag a good shake to loosen the soil in the bag.

2. Ask a grown-up to cut away three square holes—there are usually marks on the bag that act as a guide.

3. Make three small holes in the soil with your trowel or hand, ready for the plants.

Preparing a Pot:

4. Use a **10** inch (25 cm) pot or hanging basket (you will need a liner for the basket). Fill these with potting mix. Make one hole in the middle.

Planting Out

Your young tomato plants are ready to plant out now.

Top Tip!

The fruit from bush tomato plants may trail on the ground. To help keep them free from disease, plant them higher up in pots or hanging baskets.

▲ These bush tomatoes tumble down the sides of the hanging basket as they grow.

Step-by-Step

1. Take one of your plants. Gently take hold of it by the stem and pull it out of its pot, being careful not to damage its roots.

18

2. Place the plant into the hole you made earlier, in your growbag or pot. Gently but firmly press the soil around the plant.

3. Plant a second and third tomato plant in this way in a growbag. You will need to leave about 16 inches (40 cm) of space between each plant, to give them room to grow properly.

4. With a sharp pencil, poke holes along both ends of the growbag, and in between the plants. This allows water to drain out, so the soil does not get too soggy.

Top Tip!

If you only want two plants, you could use the central space of the growbag to sink an empty plant pot. Keep this filled up with water in order to keep the soil moist for the two plants at either end of the growbag.

Tending Your Crop

Check your tomato plants every day—the healthier they are, the better the harvest.

> ▶ If the soil is dry on top but still soggy underneath, do not water yet.

When to Water

Check to see if your plants need watering by pushing your fingers into the soil. If the soil is dry, you need to water the plants.

While you are watering, have a good look at your plant. Remove any dead leaves and keep an eye out for problems (see pages 22–23).

> ▶ When you water your tomato plants, you're sure to notice the strong scent they give off.

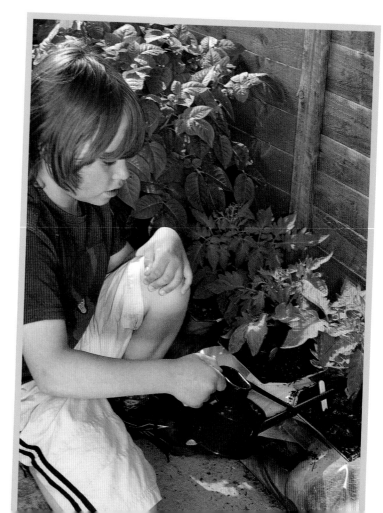

Give Support

The tall cordon varieties need a garden stake to help them grow upright. Push the stake into the soil close to the plant. To help you see the top of the cane when you are watering, stick some brightly colored adhesive tape to the top. Be careful not to poke your eyes!

Gently attach a tie to the stem of the plant and the stake in one or two places.

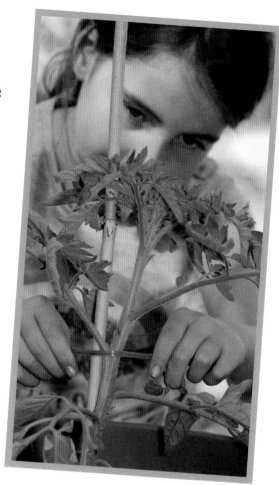

▶ You can buy plant ties at your local garden center, or use food bag ties or thick string.

Pinch Out

On tall varieties, pinch out (or take off) the main stem that starts to grow above the fourth truss, or cluster of flowers. If the plant is left to grow tall, any fruit would struggle to **ripen**.

SCIENCE SPOT *Leaves*
Don't pull off all of the leaves (right). The leaves do the hard work of turning sunlight, water, and **carbon dioxide** into a store of energy to help the plant grow. This process is called photosynthesis.

▲ Removing side-shoots also helps the plants concentrate on growing fruit.

21

Problem Page!

A lot of problems with growing tomatoes come from watering—either too much or too little. If you tend them well and every day, then you may avoid many of the problems.

▲ Tomato plants do not like their leaves to be wet all the time. If the weather is bad, try to cover them in some way.

Water Carefully!

Irregular watering—not watering for a long time and then watering a lot—can lead to **blossom end rot** (see opposite) or cause the tomatoes to swell and split. Underwatering may make your plant lose its flowers and fruit. Overwatering can make fruit lose flavor.

▶ You can tell a lot about the health of the plant by looking at its leaves. If they look healthy, your plant will be healthy, too.

◀ This plant's leaves show that it is unwell. It may have been overwatered.

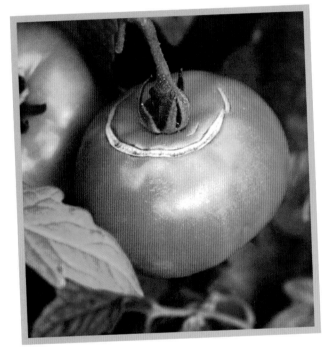

◀ This tomato has split because the soil dried out and then too much water was given all at once, making the fruit swell too quickly.

Blossom End Rot

Blossom end rot turns the end of the tomato (where the blossom was) brown. It can be caused by irregular watering and allowing your plants to dry out.

Tomato Blight

Tomatoes, like potatoes, can get **blight**. This is a disease that turns the leaves and fruit brown. It is more common in very wet weather.

◀ If your tomatoes get blight, it is best to get rid of any infected plants and fruit.

Getting Ready for Harvest

It won't be long now until all your hard work will pay off.

Green Tomatoes

Your plants probably already have some bright yellow flowers. You will soon notice small, green tomatoes begin to develop in place of your flowers. In a few weeks, they will grow and ripen in the sun.

▲ Once you have flowers, keep an eye out for the first tomato fruits.

◀ ▼ It's very exciting when you see your first fruits.

SCIENCE SPOT *Pollination*

Pollination is a process where **pollen** from the flower of one plant is transferred to another plant of the same type. This allows the plant to grow fruits and seeds to make new plants. Tomato plants are self-fertilizing, meaning that they can grow fruit without needing pollen to be taken from one plant to another by a visiting insect.

Feed Your Plants

You will need to feed any plants in pots or growbags with tomato fertilizer. Ask your grown-up helper to do this with you. Be sure to follow instructions, but start when the first small fruits have appeared.

Red and Ripe

When the tomatoes are red (if they are a red variety!), they are ripe and ready to pick. To get your tomatoes at their best and with the most flavor, pick them as soon as they turn red.

▲ You can buy tomato fertilizer from a garden center.

◀ Tomatoes are ready to harvest when they come away from the stalk easily when you pull gently.

▶ Those tiny seeds you planted 20 weeks ago are now ripe tomatoes in your hands. Enjoy!

Tasty Tomatoes

Tomatoes are a tasty food that can be enjoyed in many ways. They are good for you too! Tomatoes are rich in **vitamins** A and C. Both help the body to stay healthy and fight off infection.

Preparing Your Tomatoes

Before you get creative with your tomatoes, you need to give them a good wash in cold water. If you're not going to eat them right away, it's best to store them in the refrigerator, but tomatoes are best eaten at room temperature for flavor.

Many Uses

Can you imagine french fries without ketchup or a bacon, lettuce, and tomato sandwich without the tomatoes? Tomatoes are used in many recipes. Why not try the recipe opposite, or search the Internet for more ideas?

◀ *Tomatoes can be part of a quick snack, a sauce, or a main meal.*

Tomato Sauce

Ingredients

- 2 pounds (1 kg) tomatoes, chopped
- 1 small onion, sliced
- 2 tablespoons (25 g) brown sugar
- 1 cup vinegar (or cider vinegar)
- 1 teaspoon allspice
- 1 teaspoon salt
- 1 tablespoon paprika
- 1 teaspoon white pepper

Method

Ask an adult to help you with the chopping and cooking parts.

1. With your adult helper, simmer the tomatoes and onions over medium heat until soft.

2. Press the mixture through a sieve, then place it back into the pan and add the sugar, vinegar, spices, and so on.

3. Let it bubble until the mixture is very thick. Remember to keep stirring to stop the sauce from sticking to the bottom of the pan, especially once it starts to get thicker!

4. Pour the sauce into **sterilized** bottles and put the top on.

This should make about 2 cups (500 ml) of tomato sauce.

▶ *You could eat your tomato sauce with fries or put it on a pizza base!*

Gardening Calendar

Here's an "at-a-glance" guide to the growing year. Planting and growing times vary, depending on where you live, but you can follow these general guidelines.

Sow or plant	Tend / Prepare	Harvest
	Late Winter (Jan–Feb) Plan your crop; choose your tomato varieties.	
Sow seeds in pots on windowsills indoors in the middle of this period.	**Early Spring** (March–April) Check and water seedlings regularly.	
Begin to harden off seedlings.	**Late Spring** (April–May) Water, weed, and feed plants. Stake any tall, cordon varieties.	
Plant seedlings out at beginning of this period.	**Early Summer** (June–July) Water, weed, and feed plants.	First tomatoes will be ready for harvesting at the end of this period.
	Late Summer (July–Aug)	Plants will continue to fruit throughout this period.
	Early Fall (Sept–Oct)	Plants will fruit through to mid fall.
	Late Fall (Oct–Nov) Dig plot over, digging in compost or manure.	

Gardening Glossary

blight: a disease that affects plants, making them produce rot.

blossom end rot: a disease that turns one end of a tomato (the flower end) brown.

carbon dioxide: a gas that is part of the air around us.

conditions: the situation or surroundings that affect something.

diseases: illnesses that can be caught by plants and animals.

fertilizer: a substance such as manure or a chemical mixture used to make soil more fertile (better for growing plants).

germinate: the point when a root and leaf break through a seed case and the seed begins to grow.

growbag: a specially made plastic bag full of potting mix for growing plants in.

hardy: able to survive under poor or extreme weather.

plant on: when you move seedlings or plants from one growing place to another in order to give them more space to grow.

pollen: the powder from a flower that is needed to complete the fertilization process.

potting mix: a mixture of soil and rotted plants used to fertilize, or feed, plants to help them grow.

ripen: when a fruit is fully formed and ready to be picked.

root: the part of a plant below the ground that takes water and nutrients, or goodness, from the soil to the rest of the plant.

seed: a tiny thing that a plant can grow from.

seedling: the young plant grown from a seed.

sheltered: in this case, a spot that is out of the wind.

shoot: new growth from a plant or seed.

sterilized: glass bottles can be sterilized (made free from bacteria) by putting them in very hot water, followed by the oven. This should be done by an adult.

truss: a group, or cluster, of flowers.

varieties: different types of the same plant family.

vitamin: natural substances in food that are good for your body and health.

Index

Useful Web Sites

www.kidsgardening.org/
The National Gardening Association believes that when you garden you grow. Their comprehensive gardening resource web site for children is highly inspirational.

http://home.howstuffworks.com/ tomatoes1.htm
Information about growing your own tomatoes, with handy tips and recipes.

www.bbc.co.uk/digin/tomato.shtml
Fun, animated clip on how to grow tomatoes from seed.

Gardening Club

Have you enjoyed growing your own? How about joining a gardening club? Your school may have one. You could grow fruit and vegetables, or perhaps make ladybug homes to help attract them to your garden. If your school doesn't have a gardening club, why not talk to your teacher about setting one up?

Note to parents and teachers: Every effort has been made by the Publishers to ensure that these web sites are suitable for children, that they are of the highest educational value, and that they contain no inappropriate or offensive material. However, because of the nature of the Internet, it is impossible to guarantee that the contents of these sites will not be altered. We strongly advise that Internet access is supervised by a responsible adult.